A Year of Birds

A Year of Birds

POEMS BY

IRIS MURDOCH

ENGRAVINGS BY

REYNOLDS STONE

COMPTON PRESS

Text © Iris Murdoch 1978
Illustrations © Reynolds Stone 1978
First published 1978 by The Compton Press Ltd
The Old Brewery, Tisbury, Wiltshire
ISBN 0 900193 68 9
Designed by Humphrey Stone
This limited edition of 350 copies
was set in Monotype Dante and
printed on Zerkall mould made paper
during the autumn of 1978 at Compton Press
This copy is number

272

Iris Murdoch
Reynolds Stone

A Year of Birds

JANUARY

Inland seagulls never cry *ai-ai, ai-ai,*
But silently in winter trail
Behind the plough their kite tail.
Without a sound they pass me by
As pale as paper in the white winter sky.
Oh why do they never cry
Ai-ai, ai-ai?

FEBRUARY

Burly at dawn on the bare high
Arched articulated beech tree silhouette
With the streaming sky scarcely a pale gold
Some forty rooks sit tails all one way
Beside old nests storm proofed last spring.
Chat Chat their sitting cry; then off to work they fly
In sudden flapping spirals *Caw Caw Caw*.

MARCH

In dreadful light March evenings when the violets stain
Decorous collared doves complain complain
With black by Aphrodite ribboned necks.
Pretty pink birds so ill at ease
Raucous in our still naked trees
Spring makes you tell us love is pain, is pain.

APRIL

Moorhen shy and alert walking on a grass path
Long-legged among daffodils before the swallows.
Nothing to smell upon this chill air.
Over the pearly grass your early shadow follows.
How timidly in the dew there you peer about and start.
Rosy and yellow the April willow. Pain in the heart.

MAY

Now in the park white cricketers and cuckoo calls.
How like confetti the wild cherry falls.
Cool buds of May still keep the rose concealed.
Hollow as a flute the bird's hoot across the field.

JUNE

Black and white magpie from a Chinese picture
Flies slowly like a helicopter
On our midsummer frieze.
Night scarcely dims the daylight hours,
Long red transparent stems of roses arch with flowers
And with the curious clambering of bees.

JULY

Blackbird digging in the warm mown grass
Glancing about with an eye of glass,
Blackbird digging in the mown grass heap
How mechanical you look,
Flirting and glistening in agitation.
Quiet now yellow beak motionlessly listening
For tiny little things their doomed crepitation.

AUGUST

Over the wispy yellow slopes of the motorway
The August traveller released to holiday
Sees suddenly air-perched and perilous
Its motionless meditation aloof near the terrible tarmac
The oh so frail eternal hovering kestrel.

SEPTEMBER

Skies are a milder azure, night has a colder finger,
Bland the days linger but they are weary of summer,
And the warmth is quietly withdrawn from the long evenings.
The up-tailed wren precious invisibly piping,
Then moving like a mouse in the dusty hedgerow,
Somehow reminds us that autumn has come already.

OCTOBER

The October water is like glass and hardly flows.
Beside the red tree the swan spreads a long wing.
Rose hips too are reflected in the stream
Where the bird's sudden movement has made no sound.

NOVEMBER

The little paws of shrewmice shudder
When flies the stooping owl over
Who shrieks to make his victim stir.
Then rise up flurry wings and long tail drooping
In feathers fast asleep the fur.

DECEMBER

When the dark hawberries hang down and drip like blood
And the old man's beard has climbed up high in the wood
And the golden bracken has been broken by the snows
And Jesus Christ has come again to heal and pardon,
Then the little robin follows me through the garden,
In the dark days his breast is like a rose.